CW00508163

Autism is my SUPERPOWER

Written and Illustrated by Cecily M. Forde

Autism is my Superpower
Copyright © 2020 by Cecily Forde
All rights reserved.

This book or any portion thereof may not be reproduced or used in any manner whatsoever without the express written permission of the publisher except for the use of brief quotations in a book review.

Printed in the United States of America

ISBN: 9798649922982

Tiny Steps Publishing

tinystepspublishing.com

For Aamir,
May you always know the power that you possess.
Tiny steps lead to big strides.

Hi my name is Jacob and I have Autism. My brain thinks in a *super special* way. I want to tell you how I turn my Autism into my SUPERPOWER.

Can you guess my first SUPERPOWER?

With my SUPER SENSORY POWER I can usually hear, smell, and taste things that most people just ignore. My powers are so strong that I normally crave **BIG** hugs and squeezes to keep me calm. I can jump on my trampoline if my SUPER SENSORY POWERS are too much for me to handle.

I hear sounds all around me.
There are sounds that I like and
some that I don't.

WHOOSH

TWEET

TWEET

BOING

BOING

BUZZ

BUZZ

Can you name the different sounds in this picture?

Can you guess my next **SUPERPOWER?**

My SUPER MEMORY POWER helps my brain remember small details for a very long time. I can memorize my favorite movie, songs, and phrases. I can also remember many details about my favorite things. I like to recite my memories for fun.

CHOO CHOO

Trains are one of my favorite things.

Do you know what sound a train makes?

Can you guess my next SUPERPOWER?

My PATTERN POWER helps me remember my routines. Routines are SUPER important to me. I like knowing what comes next in every situation. I always stick to my routine. I like for everyone around me to stick to their same routine too.

Changes in routine can sometimes cause confusion.

I can remember what is coming next with
the help of my visual schedule .
Can you name the items on my visual?

Can you guess my next **SUPERPOWER?**

NUMBER POWER

With my **NUMBER POWER** ability I can solve any problem! When I enter a room full of people, I feel worried. Then, I use my **SUPERPOWER** to count the people that are in the room. I can memorize each person by the number that I give them in my head. Numbers make me feel better.

I like to count the clouds in the sky.

Can you name the different numbers in this picture?

There are **SUPERPOWERS** in all of us. We are all special in our own way.

Autism is my SUPERPOWER!

What's yours?

_____'s

SUPERPOWER

is

Printed in Great Britain
by Amazon

60912887R00015